Really Fun For Everyone

Easter Coloring Book

Volume 1

Benjamin Star

This really fun
Easter Coloring Book
Belongs to:

Really Fun For Everyone Easter Coloring Book

Volume 1

Really Fun For Everyone
Easter Coloring Book
Volume 1

Really Fun For Everyone
Easter Coloring Book
Volume 1

Really Fun For Everyone
Easter Coloring Book
Volume 1

Really Fun For Everyone
Easter coloring Book
Volume 1

Really Fun For Everyone
Easter Coloring Book
Volume 1

Really Fun For Everyone
Easter Coloring Book
volume 1

Really Fun For Everyone
Easter Coloring Book
Volume 1

Really Fun For Everyone
Easter coloring Book
volume 1

Really Fun For Everyone
Easter Coloring Book
Volume 1

Really Fun For Everyone
Easter Coloring Book
volume 1

Really Fun For Everyone
Easter Coloring Book
Volume 1

Really Fun For Everyone
Easter Coloring Book
Volume 1

Really Fun For Everyone
Easter Coloring Book
volume 1

Really Fun For Everyone
Easter Coloring Book
Volume 1

Really Fun For Everyone
Easter Coloring Book
Volume 1

Really Fun For Everyone
Easter Coloring Book
Volume 1

Really Fun For Everyone
Easter Coloring Book
volume 1

Really Fun For Everyone
Easter Coloring Book
Volume 1

Really Fun For Everyone
Easter Coloring Book
Volume 1

Really Fun For Everyone
Easter Coloring Book
Volume 1

Really Fun For Everyone
Easter Coloring Book
Volume 1

Really Fun For Everyone
Easter Coloring Book
Volume 1

Really Fun For Everyone
Easter Coloring Book
Volume 1

Really Fun For Everyone
Easter Coloring Book
Volume 1

Really Fun For Everyone
Easter Coloring Book
Volume 1

Really Fun For Everyone
Easter Coloring Book
volume 1

Really Fun For Everyone
Easter Coloring Book
volume 1

Really Fun For Everyone
Easter Coloring Book
volume 1

Really Fun For Everyone
Easter Coloring Book
volume 1

Really Fun For Everyone
Easter Coloring Book
Volume 1

Really Fun For Everyone
Easter Coloring Book
Volume 1

Really Fun For Everyone
Easter Coloring Book
volume 1

Really Fun For Everyone
Easter Coloring Book
Volume 1

Really Fun For Everyone
Easter Coloring Book
volume 1

Really Fun For Everyone
Easter Coloring Book
Volume 1

Really Fun For Everyone
Easter Coloring Book
volume 1

Really Fun For Everyone
Easter Coloring Book
volume 1

Really Fun For Everyone
Easter Coloring Book
Volume 1

Really Fun For Everyone
Easter coloring Book
volume 1

Really Fun For Everyone
Easter Coloring Book
Volume 1

Really Fun For Everyone
Easter coloring Book
volume 1

Really Fun For Everyone
Easter Coloring Book
volume 1

Really Fun For Everyone
Easter Coloring Book
Volume 1

Really Fun For Everyone
Easter Coloring Book
volume 1

Really Fun For Everyone
Easter Coloring Book
Volume 1

Really Fun For Everyone
Easter Coloring Book
volume 1

Really Fun For Everyone
Easter Coloring Book
volume 1